Fairy Tale Ca

Crown & Wand, pg. 44

Carriage, pg. 35

Castle, pg. 2

mary maxim

Mary Maxim, Inc. 2001 Holland Ave., Port Huron, MI 48060 • www.marymaxim.com
Mary Maxim, LLC. 75 Scott Ave., Paris, ON N3L 3G5 • www.marymaxim.ca

LEISURE ARTS, INC. • Maumelle, Arkansas

Fairy Tale Castle

SHOPPING LIST

- ☐ Worsted weight yarn (refer to master key below)
- ☐ Tapestry Needle #18
- ☐ 2- 3" Plastic Canvas Circles
- ☐ 12- Clear 7 Mesh Ultra Stiff Plastic Canvas 13.5" x 22"
- ☐ 2- 8mm Fuchsia Beads
- ☐ 2- 3/16" Dowels 6" long
- ☐ 3" x 3" Pink Felt
- ☐ 3" x 3" Lavender Felt

SIZE:

24" x 7" x 14.5" [61 x 18 x 37 cm]

Please read all instructions included on page 48 before beginning.

INSTRUCTIONS:

This project has a lot of pieces and several are very similar. You may want to cut out just the pieces you'll be working according to the instructions.

Refer to layout diagrams (pgs. 7 & 8) to fit pieces as needed on plastic canvas sheets.

1. Using brown, work the two areas as shown on the exterior base piece (pg. 9). Overcast the edges of these areas between the triangles.

2. Work the exterior left (pgs. 10 & 11) and exterior right (pgs. 12 & 13) tower pieces. Using medium pink, overcast the edges of both pieces between all 3 triangles.

See the window lattice guides (pg. 10) to work the white long stitches on each of the windows. Work

these stitches in one direction only at first. When working the stitches in the other direction, carefully pass the needle under alternating stitches to create a basket weave effect. White stitches are to be worked over the purple stitches.

Using lavender, work and overcast all edges of four large exterior window frames (pg. 11) and 14 tiny window frames (pg. 11). Using lavender, tack a window frame onto each window area of the two tower pieces.

3. Work the left exterior front, left bump out (pg. 13), exterior lower center, right bump out and right exterior front pieces (pg. 14). Work the white long stitches on the window areas.

Using lavender, work and overcast 2 small window frames (pg. 11). Tack the frames to the windows.

Using medium pink, join the two bump out pieces to the exterior lower center and to the two exterior front pieces (matching up the letters).

4. Work the exterior center left and exterior center right trim pieces (pg. 12).
Using light pink, join the left trim to the left exterior front and the right trim to the right exterior front between the triangles.

Using light pink, join each trim piece to the exterior lower center between the triangles.

Using medium pink, join the rest of each of these rows from the triangle to the Z.

Using medium pink, overcast the bottom edge of both trims. Overcast the exterior left front from Z to B and the left bump out from B to C. Overcast the exterior right bump out from E to G and the exterior right front from G to Z. Overcast the exterior lower center from Z to C and E to Z.

5. Form a circle with the upper section of the exterior right tower piece and use medium pink to join the edges from A to B. Repeat with the exterior left tower joining from C to D.

Matching the orange dots, attach an unworked exterior tower top piece (pg. 12) to the top edge of each exterior tower piece.

Master Key

╱	Lt. Pink - 176 yds
╱	Med. Pink - 166 yds
╱	Dk. Pink - 134 yds
╱	Lavender - 284 yds
╱	Purple - 234 yds
╱	Grey - 104 yds
╱	Tan - 86 yds
╱	Brown - 38 yds
╱	Dk. Green - 24 yds
╱	Lt. Green - 98 yds
╱	White - 24 yds
╱	Gold - 6 yds
—	Joining Line

Join the exterior left tower to the left exterior front from I to K and overcast the left exterior front from K to O. Join the exterior right tower to the right exterior front from L to M and overcast the right exterior front from M to O.

Using medium pink, start to join the bottom edge of the exterior right tower piece to the exterior base piece at the X's. Join these pieces until you reach the O, but don't end this piece of yarn, you may need to make some adjustments in your stitching.

Join the bottom edge of the exterior lower center piece to the base from N to F. Join the right bump out and the right exterior front to the base at matching letters. Finish joining the tower to the base, adjusting if necessary.

Repeat to join the left exterior tower pieces to the opposite side of the base matching up the letters.

6. Work the heart shaped piece (pg. 11). Overcast all edges with purple.

Using dark pink, attach the top half of the heart to the exterior lower center piece (see joining lines).

The lower half of the heart will be used to keep the draw bridge door closed.

7. Work two tower trim pieces, 8 small and 8 large tower roof pieces (pg. 15) in purple half cross stitch. Overcast both long side edges of all roof pieces with purple.

Using lavender, work the long stitches on all of the 16 roof pieces as shown.

Using purple, tack a large and a

small tower roof piece from X to O. Alternating sizes, join 3 more large and 3 more small tower roof pieces to create a cone shaped roof.

Do not stitch the top point closed, leaving room for the flagpole.

Join a tower trim piece to the bottom edges of this roof assembly. Join the short edges of the tower trim piece together and overcast all unworked edges with purple.

Cut out the hole in the center of the flag pole support (pg. 15). Insert an unworked flagpole support piece into the tower roof, keep it level and tack in place. Center this roof on top of one tower and tack in place. Repeat to create & attach the second tower roof.

8. Work the interior left tower (pg. 16) and the interior right tower (pg. 17) pieces. Work the window lattice. Using medium pink, work and overcast four large window frames (pg. 11). Tack a frame on each window.

Using light pink, join the two short edges of the top unworked area of each interior tower piece together. Join an unworked interior top (pg. 18) to the top edge of each interior tower piece matching the orange dots.

Work the left and right tower ceiling pieces (pg. 18). Using matching colors, overcast each piece between the triangles (along curved edge).

Join each ceiling to the matching interior tower piece from A to triangle and from B to triangle. Tack the ceiling and tower pieces together between the triangles.

9. Work the dressing room front wall (pg. 18), right wall, left wall and ceiling pieces (pg. 19). Work the window lattice on the front wall. Using medium pink, work, overcast and tack a small window frame (pg. 11) in place.

Join the left wall to the front from A to B and to the right wall from C to D. Join the ceiling to the lower unworked row on the dressing room right wall, to the front wall, and to the left wall pieces.

10. Work the stairwell right and left wall (pg. 20) pieces. Work the stairwell front (pg. 21). Work the window lattice. Using medium pink, work, overcast and tack a small window frame (pg. 11) in place.

Using grey, work the first stair side, second stair side (pg. 20), landing, landing front and the back stair wall pieces (pg. 21). Work 6 step pieces (marked with letters [pg. 21]), and join them together along their long edges to create a long strip. Join these steps to the first stair side piece matching up the letters. Join the top step and the first stair side pieces to the landing front piece from I to A and A to H. Join the landing piece to the landing front piece from K to L. Join the steps and the landing pieces to the joining rows on the stairwell left wall.

Work and join 16 more steps together. Join one side of these steps to the second stair side piece, placing the bottom step at L to P and the top ending at O. Join the other side of these steps to the stairwell right wall piece along the joining rows.

Join the back stair wall to the stairwell right wall (along joining row), to top step and to second stair side piece from O to N. Join the second stair side piece to the landing front piece from L to M. Join the landing to the bottom step, to the stairwell right and to the stairwell front pieces along the joining rows.

Join the stairwell front to the stairwell left and right walls with light green.

Work and join the stairwell ceiling (pg. 21) to the stairwell front, left and right wall pieces.

11. Work the interior base (pg. 22), the upper deck (pg. 23), the upper room floor (pg. 24).

Work the interior left and right center walls (pgs. 24 & 25), and the interior lower center (pg. 26). Work the exterior upper center (pg. 26) and use medium pink to overcast the top edges between the triangles. Work lattice on this piece. Using lavender, work, overcast and tack a triple window frame (pg. 24) in place.

12. Using tan, join the bottom edge of the exterior upper center piece to the upper deck from A to B.

Work the upper room ceiling pieces (pg. 27). Join a ceiling piece to the top edge of the interior left center wall from A to B (ceiling piece will extend slightly beyond the edge of the wall piece). Join the other ceiling piece to the interior right center wall piece from C to D.

Work the upper room center piece (pg. 27). Using lavender, overcast the top edges of this piece (between the triangles). Work lattice on each window. Using

medium pink, work, overcast and tack a triple window frame (pg. 24) in place.
Work the entry ceiling (pg. 26) as shown. Attach the entry ceiling support (pg. 27) to the back side of the entry ceiling along the joining rows with light pink and matching the stitch direction.

Using light pink, join the entry ceiling piece to the lower unworked rows on the interior left and right center wall pieces. Using lavender, join the upper room floor to the top unworked rows of the same wall pieces.

Join the upper room ceiling pieces together (between the triangles) and tack to upper room center piece.

Using purple, work back roof trim piece (pg. 27). Join the unworked edges of ceiling to the joining rows of the trim and overcast trim between the triangles using purple. Using tan, join upper room floor to entry ceiling.

13. Using light green, join stairwell left, front and right wall pieces to the interior base.

Using grey, join all of the stair pieces to the interior base.

Using light green, join the interior right tower piece to the interior base and to the stairwell right wall.

Using lavender, join the dressing room right, front and left wall pieces to the interior base. Join the interior left tower piece to the interior base and to the dressing room left wall.

Work the two center roof pieces (pg. 28) in purple half cross stitch except for the joining rows. Using

lavender, work the long stitches on these two pieces except at the unworked rows and below. Work two side trim pieces (pg. 28) and join them to the center roof pieces along the edge closest to the unworked row. Overcast the edges of the side trim pieces between the triangles.

Join the top edge of the stairwell left wall to the unworked row on one of the center roof pieces. Join the dressing room right wall to the other roof piece. Using lavender, finish working the long stitches on the roof.

Work the front roof trim piece (pg. 28) and overcast between the triangles. Using purple, join center roof pieces together from A to B. Join front roof trim piece to the front edges of the center roof and to the side trim pieces.

14. Using light pink, join the front edge of the upper deck piece to the upper unworked row on the interior lower center piece from C to D.

Work the 13 deck trim pieces (pg. 29) as shown and use light pink for all joining. Join the interior left trim piece to the upper deck from E to F and overcast trim from F to L. Join the interior right trim piece to the upper deck from G to H and overcast trim from H to M.

Join the interior back left trim piece to the upper deck from E to J. Join the interior back right trim piece to the upper deck and to the back stair pieces from G to K. Join trim pieces together at the corners.

Join the interior left stairwell trim and interior front stairwell trim pieces together from X to Y. Join these two pieces to the stairwell ceiling and the left wall pieces.

Join the interior center left trim piece to the upper deck from C to X. Join the interior center right trim piece to the upper deck from D to X. Join trim pieces at the corners.

Join the exterior front stairwell trim to the exterior left stairwell trim from O to N and to the exterior right stairwell trim from M to L. Join these three pieces to the upper deck from Q to N and L to P.

15. Fit the upper deck onto the castle interior. Slide it between the tower ceilings and their unworked top sections.

Wrap the stairwell exterior pieces around the stairwell interior pieces. Using medium pink, join the exterior upper center piece to the stairwell left wall and the dressing room right wall.

Using tan, join the upper deck to the stairwell left wall and dressing room right wall.

Using light pink, join the upper deck to the dressing room front and stairwell front pieces. Join all edges of the interior and exterior stairwell trim pieces (and the top edges of the stairwell right wall).

16. Slide the entry/upper room assembly into the center of the castle. Using medium pink, join the bottom edges to the base.

Insert support walls (pg. 32). Join the interior left center wall to the dressing room right wall. Join the interior right center wall to the stairwell left wall. Join the interior lower center piece to the interior base, the interior left center wall and the interior right center wall.

Using purple, join back roof trim to center roof pieces and side trim pieces. Using medium pink, join all edges of the small doorway opening.

Lay the castle's exterior face down on a clean, flat surface. Start to insert the castle's interior by gently pushing the top of the light green tower into its exterior tower. Gently inset the top of the lavender tower into its exterior. Slowly and carefully slide the interior base into the castle's exterior.

17. Using light pink, join the exterior right trim to the exterior back right trim from A to B. Overcast from B to triangle. Join the exterior left trim to the exterior back left trim from C to D. Overcast from D to triangle.

Join the dressing room and the left tower ceilings to the unworked row on the exterior back left trim piece. Overcast the bottom edge of this trim piece.

Join the stairwell ceiling and the right tower ceiling to the unworked row on the exterior back right trim piece. Overcast the bottom edge of this trim piece.

Join all upper edges of interior and exterior trim pieces.

Tack the bottom edges of the exterior left and exterior right trim pieces to the exterior towers.

Tack the exterior back left and right trim pieces to the dressing room right wall and stairwell left wall.

Using medium pink, join the interior towers to the exterior towers along the back edges.

Slide the unworked base support piece (pg. 30) between the interior and exterior base pieces. Using grey, join the interior base to the exterior base across the back edge and in the draw bridge at the front.

18. Using medium pink, work two small doorway frame pieces (pg. 28) and overcast the outer edges. Work the small doorway frame edge piece (pg. 28) and join one long edge to the inner edge of one of the doorway frame pieces and other edge to the other frame piece and overcast all of the bottom edges. Slip this doorway frame into the small doorway opening and tack in place.

19. Using medium pink, join the edges of the openings of the interior and exterior lower center pieces.

Using purple, work the draw bridge interior and exterior pieces (pg. 31 [the interior piece is one row shorter than the exterior piece]). Overcast the bottom edge of the draw bridge interior piece. Separate a strand of lavender into its individual plies and using 2 plies, work the long stitches on both pieces.

Hold these pieces back to back with top and side edges even. Using purple, join these edges together and tack the bottom edge of the interior piece to the exterior piece.

Join the bottom edge of the draw bridge exterior piece to the unworked edge at the front of the exterior base from N to P.

Using lavender, work, overcast, assemble and attach the draw bridge frame (pg. 31) as you did the small doorway frame.

The longer side of the frame edge is joined to the draw bridge exterior frame.

Make a braid using 3 strands of grey yarn and measuring approximately 5" [12.7 cm] long. Set the castle on a flat surface and adjust the length of the braid so that it is straight but not tight between the O's on the draw bridge interior piece and the draw bridge exterior frame. Make a matching second braid. Attach these chains at the O's.

20. Work 4 large and 2 of each small shrub pieces and overcast their (straight) bottom edges (pg. 33).

Use 2 ply of light pink, medium pink and dark pink to make lazy daisy flowers on two of the tall shrubs and 2 different short shrubs. Using 2 ply of gold, make French knot centers on each flower.

Hold a plain shrub and a matching flowered shrub back to back and join all unworked edges. Repeat to form the other 3 shrubs. Slightly open up the base of a tall shrub and tack it to one of the brown areas of the exterior base with dark green. Repeat with a short shrub in the same area. Repeat to attach the other two shrubs to the other brown area of the base.

21. Trace the patterns (pg. 25) and use to cut 2 flags from the pink felt and 4 crowns from the purple. Glue a crown on each side of both flags. Glue the straight edge of each flag to a dowel about .5" from the top. Glue a bead on top of each dowel. Place a flag in the hole at the top of each tower.

TABLE (pg. 33):
22. Using tan, work the table top and the 4 table legs as shown. Join 2 leg pieces from A to B, join a third from C to D and the fourth from E to F. Join the fourth leg to the first from G to H.

Join the tops of the legs to the unworked table base piece at the matching letters.

Join the edge of an unworked 3" circle to the center bar of the table edge piece. Center and tack the table base to the circle.

Join the outer edge of the table top to the top edge of the table edge piece. Overcast all unworked edges.

CHAIRS
23. Work half cross stitches shown on chair pieces (pg. 32). Make 2 side leg pieces. Using 2 ply of brown, work the long stitches on seat back and back leg pieces.

Join one long edge of a seat piece to bottom edge of a seat back piece.

Join the top edge of a side leg piece to each short edge of the seat.

Join a front leg piece to the remaining edge of seat. Join the front leg piece to each side leg piece.

Join a back leg piece to the seat back and both side leg pieces.

Overcast all unworked edges including cut out areas.

Assemble 3 more chairs.

THRONES (pgs. 33 & 34):
24. Work a throne seat back piece and two throne arm pieces. Join

a throne arm top piece to each arm. Join these arm pieces to the joining rows on the seat back.

Work a throne seat piece and join it to the bottom edges of the seat back piece and the arm pieces.

Work a throne front leg piece and join it to the seat, arms and arm tops. Work two throne side pieces and join one side piece to each side of the front leg piece and to the arm top pieces.

Using gold, work the long stitches on the seat back piece.

Work the throne back leg piece. Join the back piece to the sides and to the seat back.

Using brown, overcast all unworked edges.

Repeat to make a second throne.

BED (pg. 34):
25. Work the bed top piece. Using 2 ply of gold, work the long stitches on this piece.

Work the dark pink stitches as shown on the bed end and 2 side pieces. Overcast the bottom edge of dark pink areas. Turn these pieces over and work the purple stitches on the other side of the canvas.

Using dark pink, join the bed top to the bed ends and sides on joining rows. Using purple, join the bed ends and sides together at corners.

Work the two curtain end and two curtain side pieces. Join the curtain end pieces to the curtain side pieces along their long edges.

Slide the curtain pieces down over the bed pieces.

Using tan, join these pieces together along both edges of the unworked curtain rod areas. Using purple, join the curtains together where they meet. Join the lower sections and bottom edges of the curtains to the bed ends and bed sides.

Cut a 9" [23 cm] length of gold, thread the yarn out through one of the yellow dots at an inside corner of a curtain and then across the outside edge of this corner. Thread the yarn back inward through the other yellow dot.

Both ends of the yarn should be at the inside of this corner. Remove the needle and bring a yarn end

around each edge of the curtain. Tie these ends in a knot at the outside corner of this curtain section. Repeat at the other three corners.

MIRROR (pg. 34):
26. Work the mirror back, two mirror cross bar pieces and 4 mirror leg pieces. Carefully cut out indicated areas. Using brown, join the cross bar pieces together along both long edges. Referring to photo on back cover, join the short ends of this doubled cross bar to the lower rows on the two inside leg pieces. Join an outside leg piece to the edges of each inside leg piece (back to back), join the edges of the cut outs too.

Work the mirror front piece. Hold the mirror front and back pieces back to back. Using brown, join the edges of these two pieces and overcast the unworked edges of the back piece.

Starting with the lower ends, gently push the hooks of the back piece through the openings in the leg pieces.

Layout Diagrams

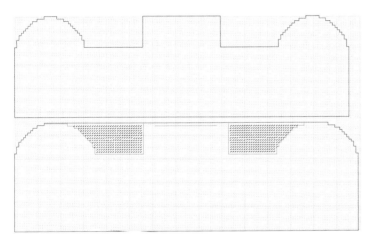
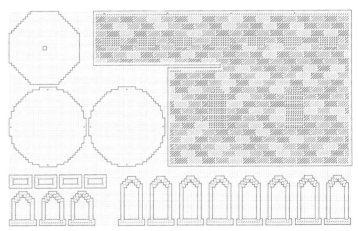
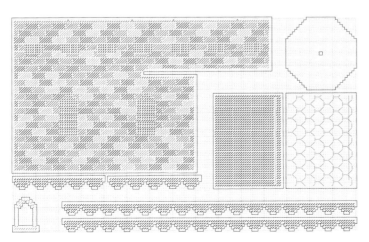
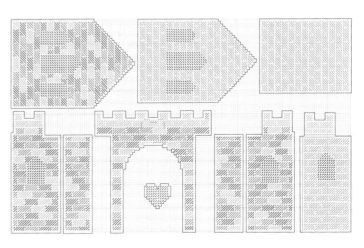

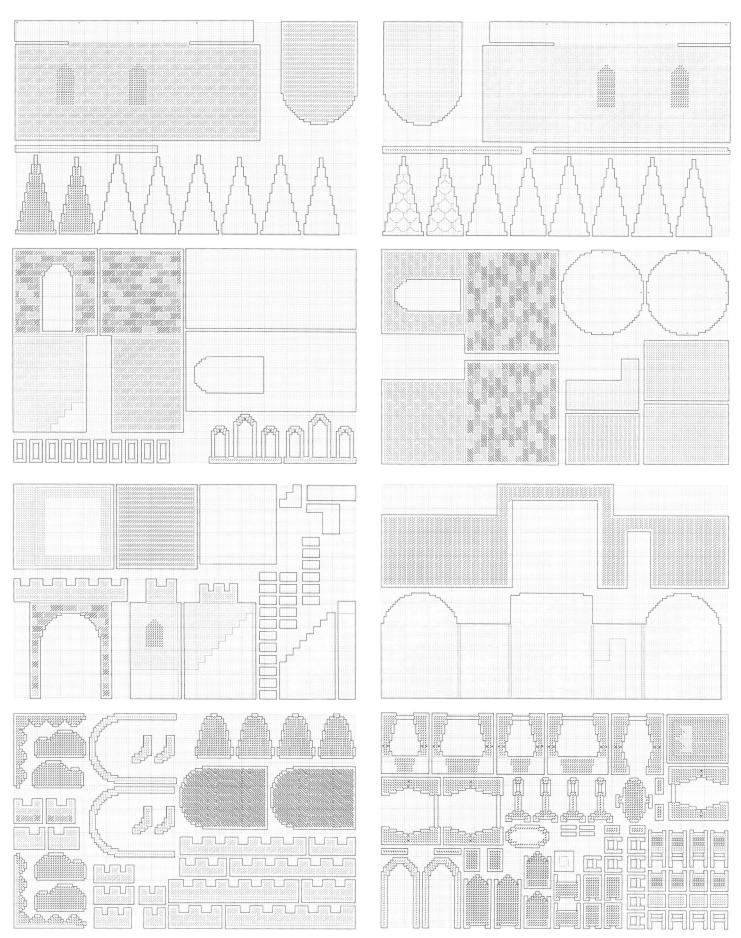

Exterior Base (150 x 46 threads)

This Exterior Base chart represents one 150 x 46 thread canvas piece. It is divided into two sections to make it large enough to be followed easily. No threads or stitches are repeated from one piece to the next.

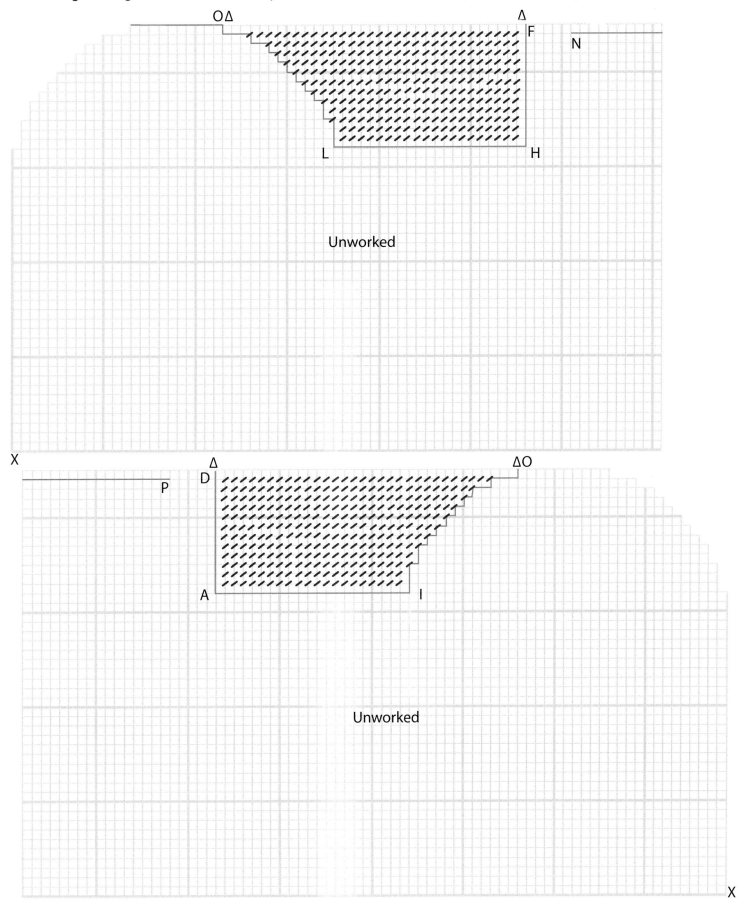

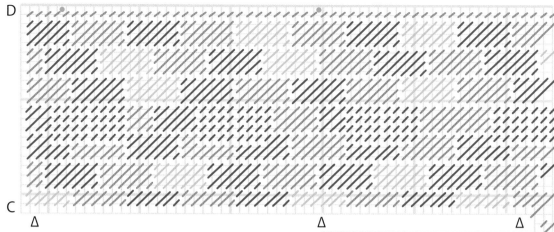

D

C

Exterior Left Tower
(114 x 66 threads)

This Exterior Left Tower chart represents one 114 x 66 thread canvas piece. It is divided across two pages to make it large enough to be followed easily. No threads or stitches are repeated from one page to the next.

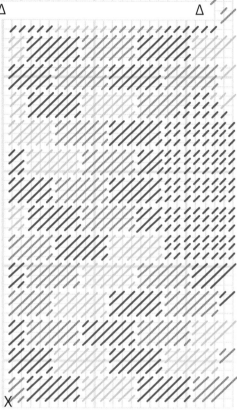

X

Large Window Lattice Guide
(10 x 19 threads)

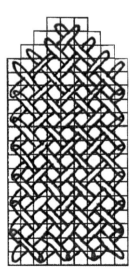

Small Window Lattice Guide
(10 x 13 threads)

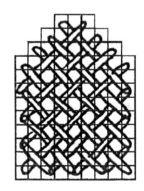

Tiny Window Lattice Guide
(10 x 6 threads)

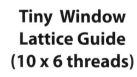

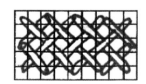

Lattice Guide for Sides of Triple Window
(8 x 14 threads)

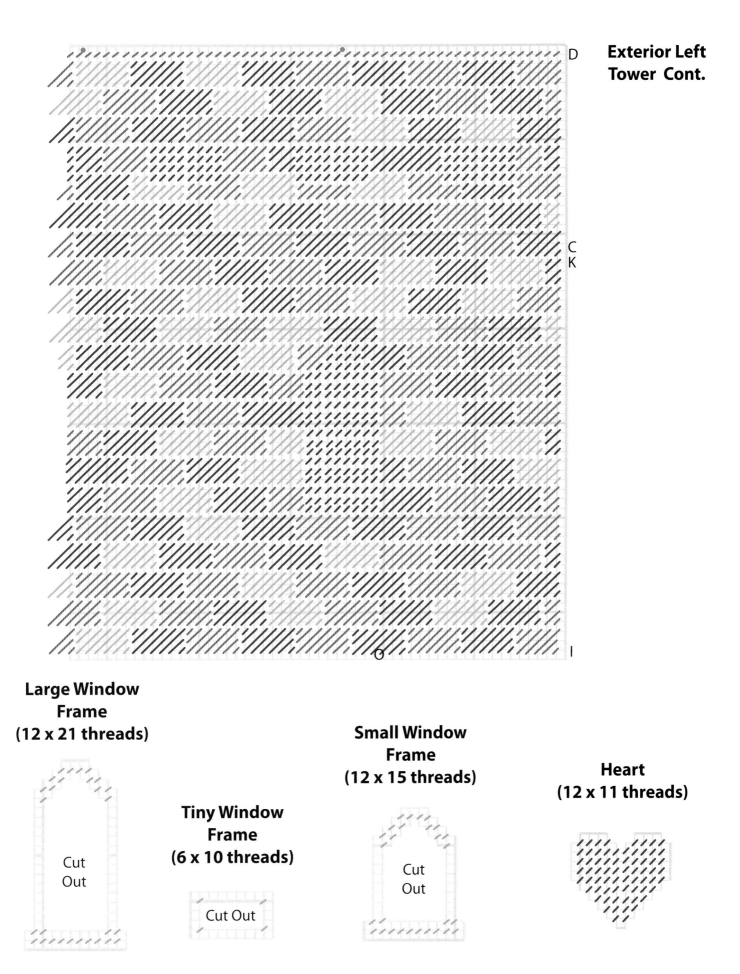

D

C
K

O

I

**Large Window
Frame
(12 x 21 threads)**

Cut
Out

**Tiny Window
Frame
(6 x 10 threads)**

Cut Out

**Small Window
Frame
(12 x 15 threads)**

Cut
Out

**Heart
(12 x 11 threads)**

Exterior Right Tower
(114 x 66 threads)

This Exterior Left Tower chart represents one 150 x 46 thread canvas piece. It is divided across two pages to make it large enough to be followed easily. No threads or stitches are repeated from one page to the next.

Exterior Tower Top
(36 x 36 threads)

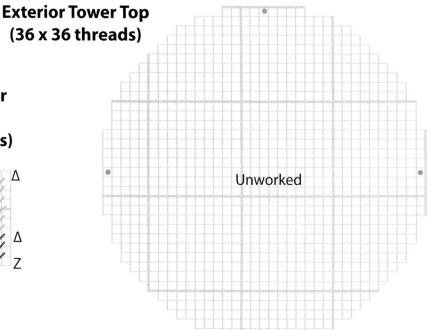

Unworked

Exterior Center Left Trim
(13 x 11 threads)

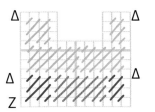

Exterior Center Right Trim
(13 x 11 threads)

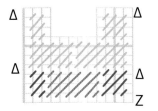

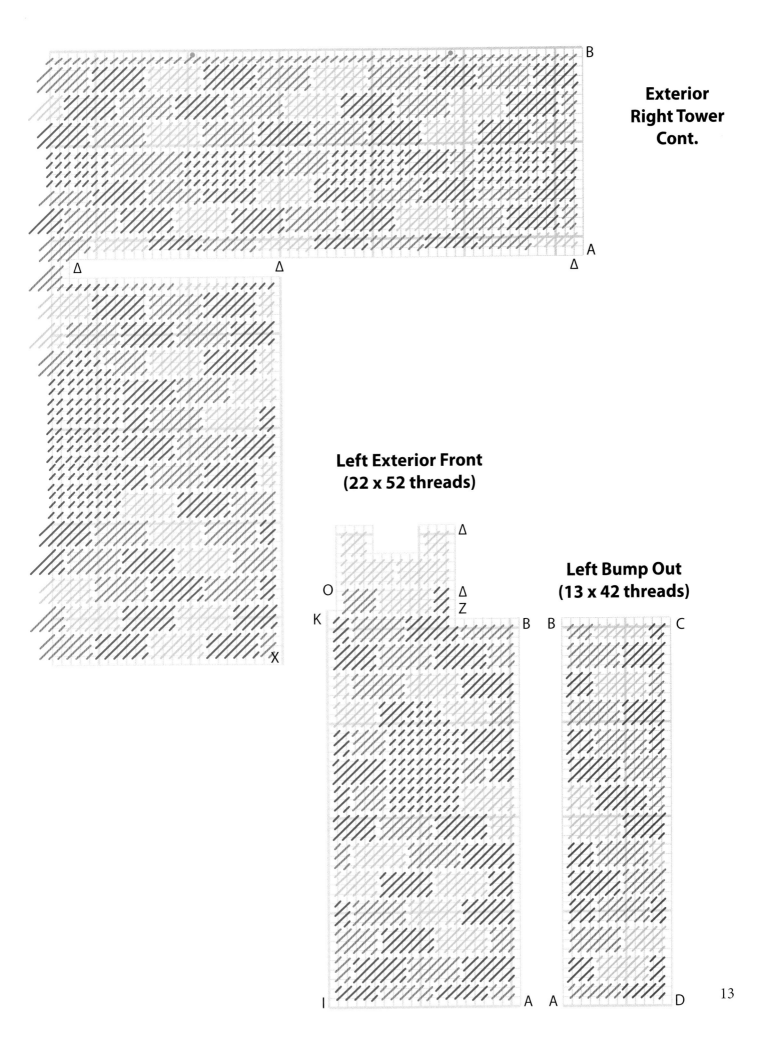

Exterior Right Tower Cont.

Left Exterior Front (22 x 52 threads)

Left Bump Out (13 x 42 threads)

13

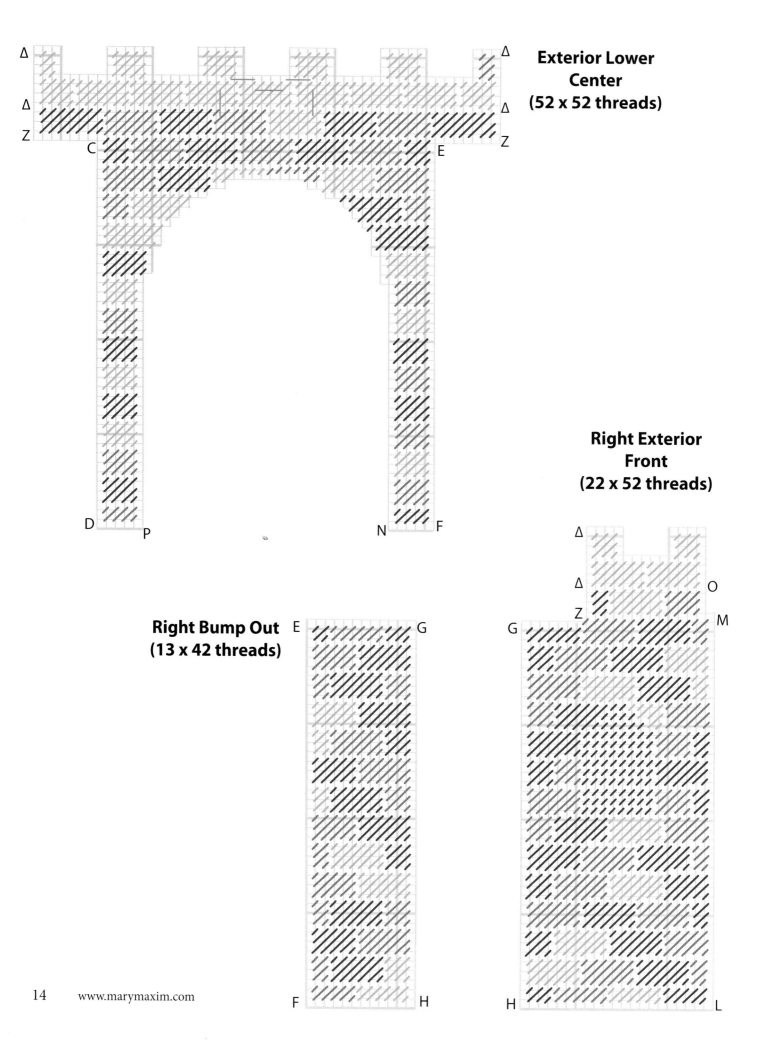

Exterior Lower Center
(52 x 52 threads)

Right Exterior Front
(22 x 52 threads)

Right Bump Out
(13 x 42 threads)

**Tower Trim
(129 x 6
threads)**

This Tower Trim chart represents one 129 x 6 thread canvas piece. It is divided into two sections to make it large enough to be followed easily. No threads or stitches are repeated from one piece to the next.

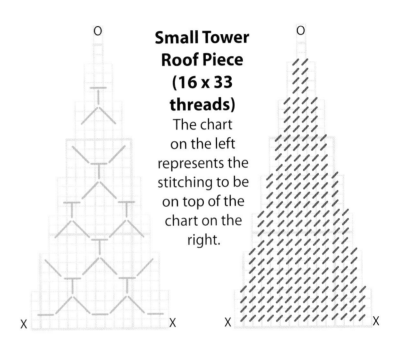

Small Tower Roof Piece (16 x 33 threads)
The chart on the left represents the stitching to be on top of the chart on the right.

Flag Pole Support (31 x 31 threads)

Unworked

Large Tower Roof Piece (18 x 34 threads)
The chart on the left represents the stitching to be on top of the chart on the right.

15

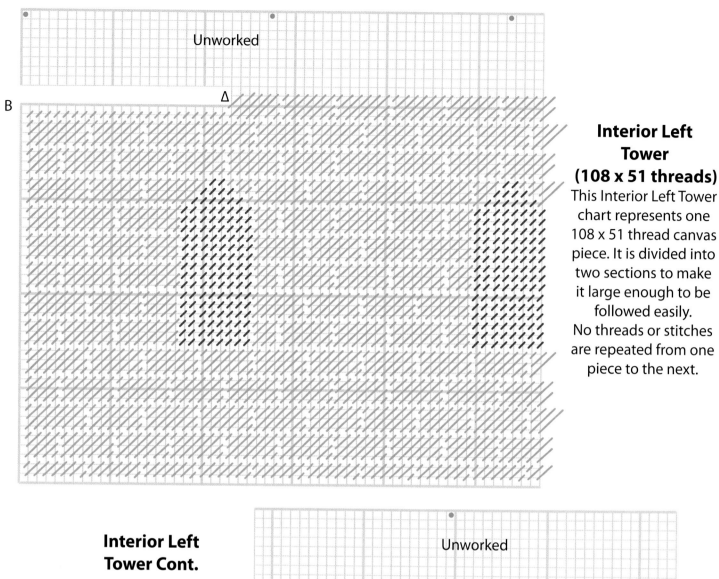

Unworked

B

Δ

Interior Left Tower
(108 x 51 threads)

This Interior Left Tower chart represents one 108 x 51 thread canvas piece. It is divided into two sections to make it large enough to be followed easily. No threads or stitches are repeated from one piece to the next.

Interior Left Tower Cont.

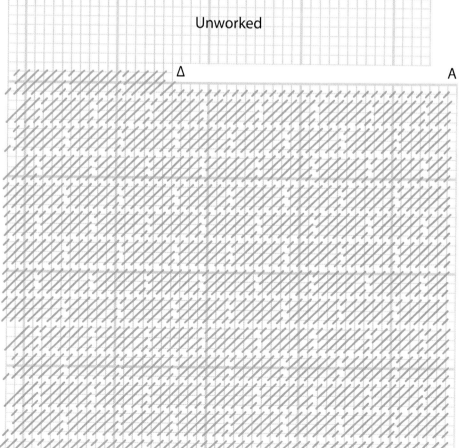

Unworked

Δ

A

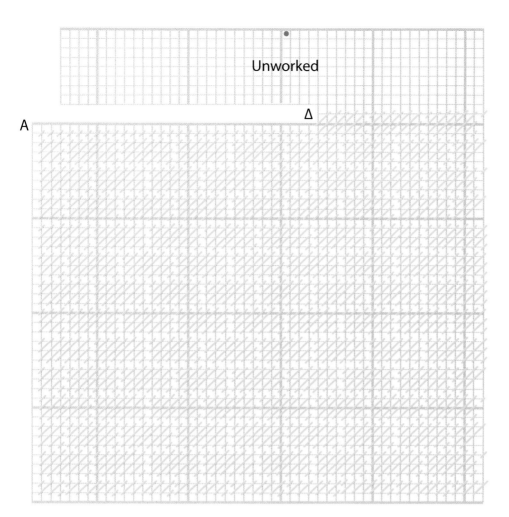

**Interior Right
Tower
(108 x 51 threads)**
This Interior Right Tower
chart represents one
105 x 51 thread canvas
piece. It is divided into
two sections to make
it large enough to be
followed easily.
No threads or stitches
are repeated from one
piece to the next.

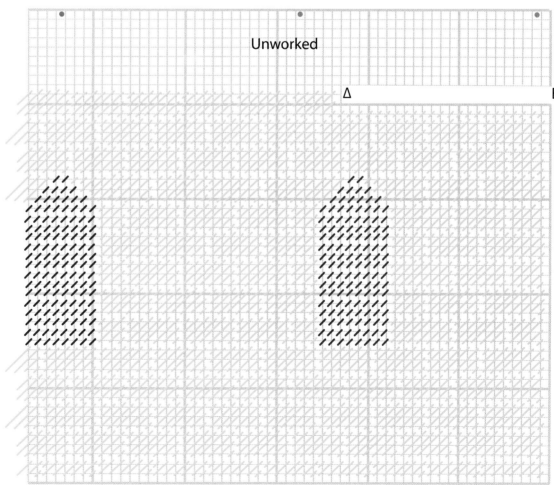

Interior Top
(34 x 34 threads)

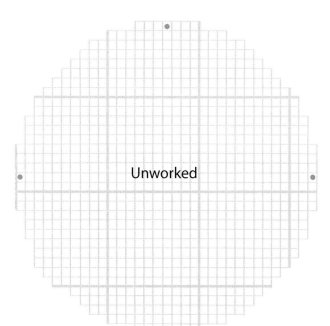

Unworked

Left Tower Ceiling
(34 x 44 threads)

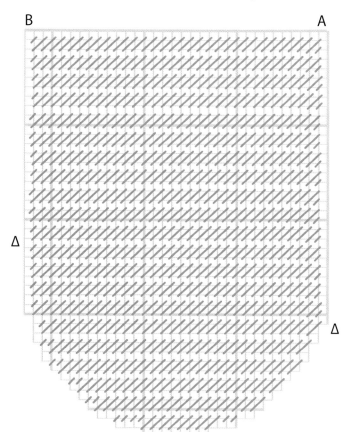

Right Tower Ceiling
(34 x 44 threads)

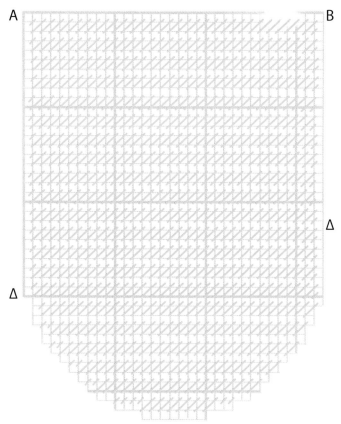

Dressing Room Front Wall
(23 x 51 threads)

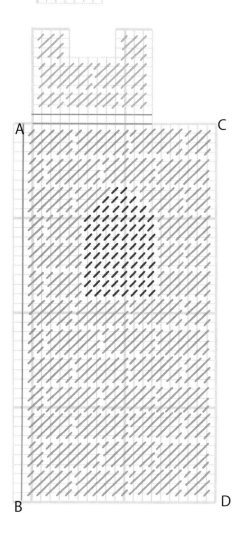

Dressing Room Left Wall
(32 x 41 threads)

Dressing Room Right Wall
(37 x 78 threads)

Dressing Room Ceiling
(22 x 32 threads)

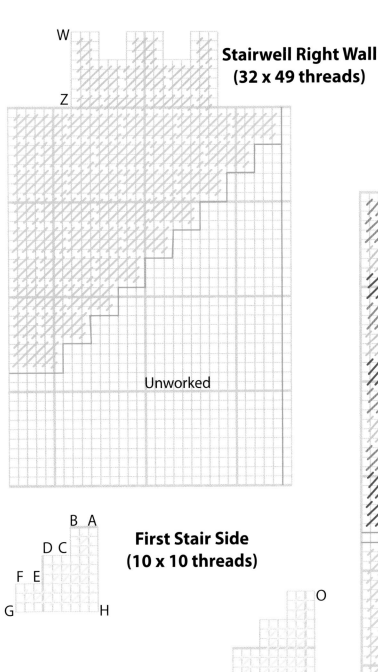

Stairwell Right Wall
(32 x 49 threads)

W

Z

Unworked

Stairwell Left Wall
(37 x 78 threads)

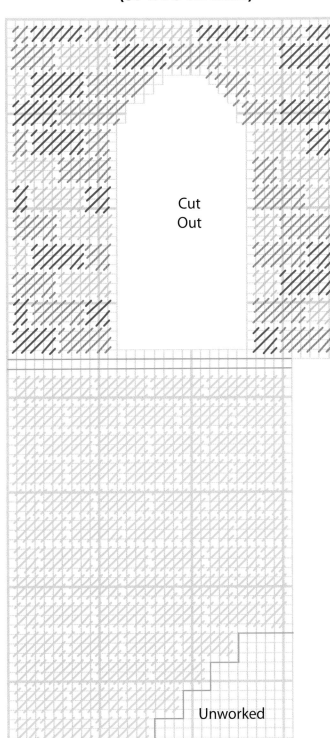

Cut
Out

Unworked

B A

First Stair Side
(10 x 10 threads)

D C

F E

G H

O

Second Stair Side
(25 x 37 threads)

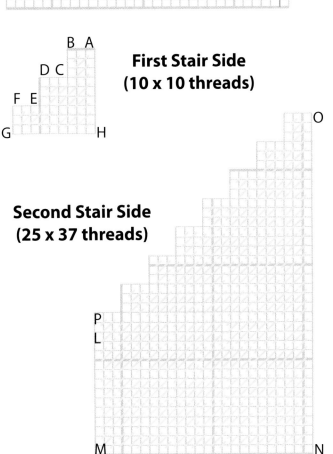

P
L

M N

Landing
(22 x 7 threads)

K   L

Landing Front
(15 x 13 threads)

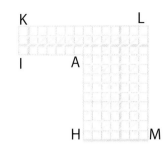

K   L
I   A
H   M

Back Stair Wall
(8 x 42 threads)

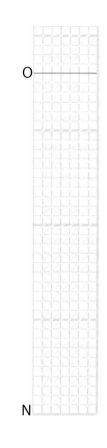

O

N

Steps
(8 x 4 threads)

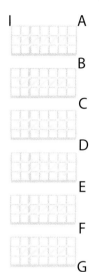

I   A
B
C
D
E
F
G

Stairwell Ceiling
(32 x 22 threads)

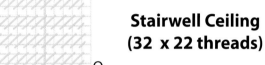

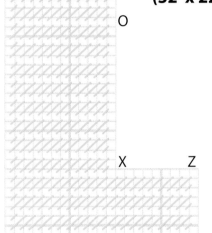

O

X   Z

Stairwell Front
(23 x 51 threads)

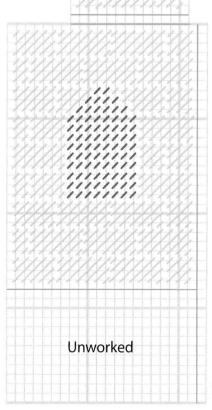

Unworked

21

Interior Base (148 x 45 threads)

This Interior Base chart represents one 148 x 45 thread canvas piece. It is divided into two sections to make it large enough to be followed easily. No threads or stitches are repeated from one piece to the next.

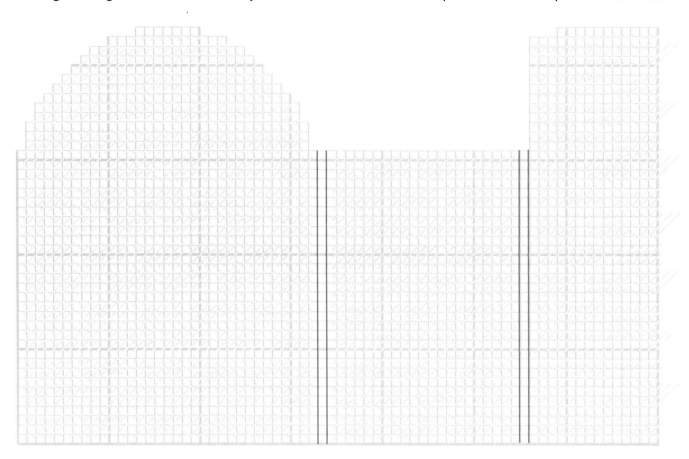

Interior Base Cont.

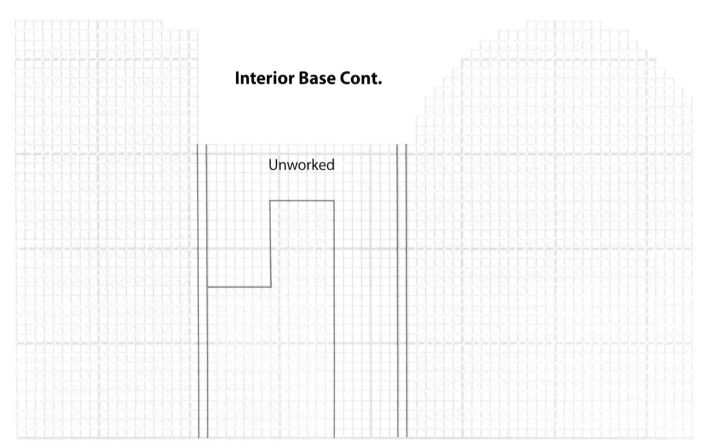

Unworked

Upper Deck (151 x 44 threads)

This Upper Deck chart represents one 151 x 44 thread canvas piece. It is divided into two sections to make it large enough to be followed easily. No threads or stitches are repeated from one piece to the next.

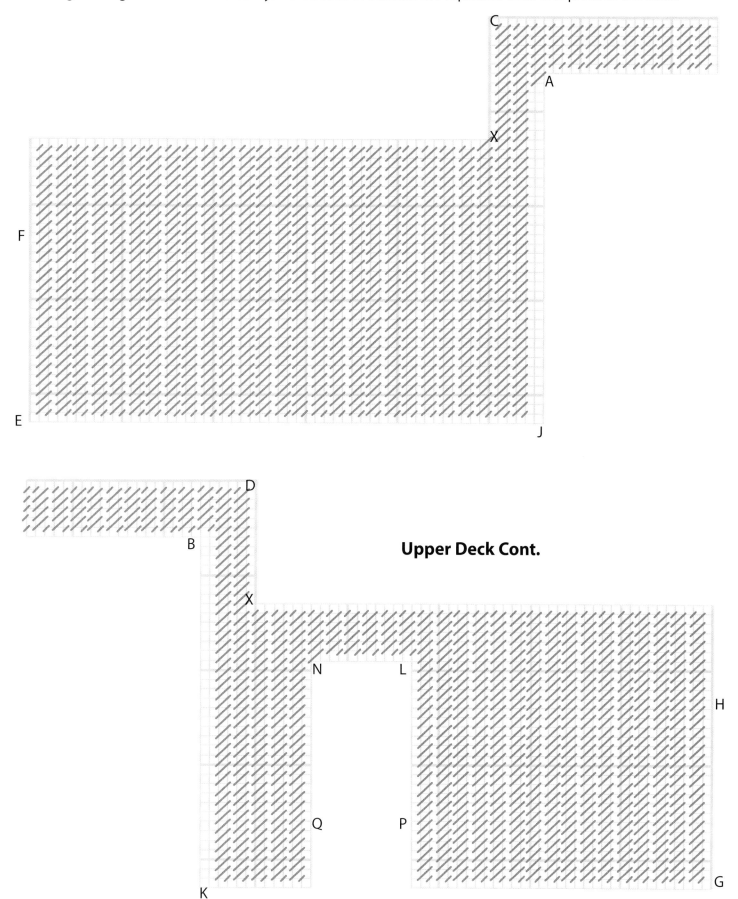

Upper Deck Cont.

Interior Left
Center Wall
(44 x 77 threads)

Upper Room Floor
(36 x 36 threads)

A   B

E

Triple Window
Frame
(32 x 21 threads)

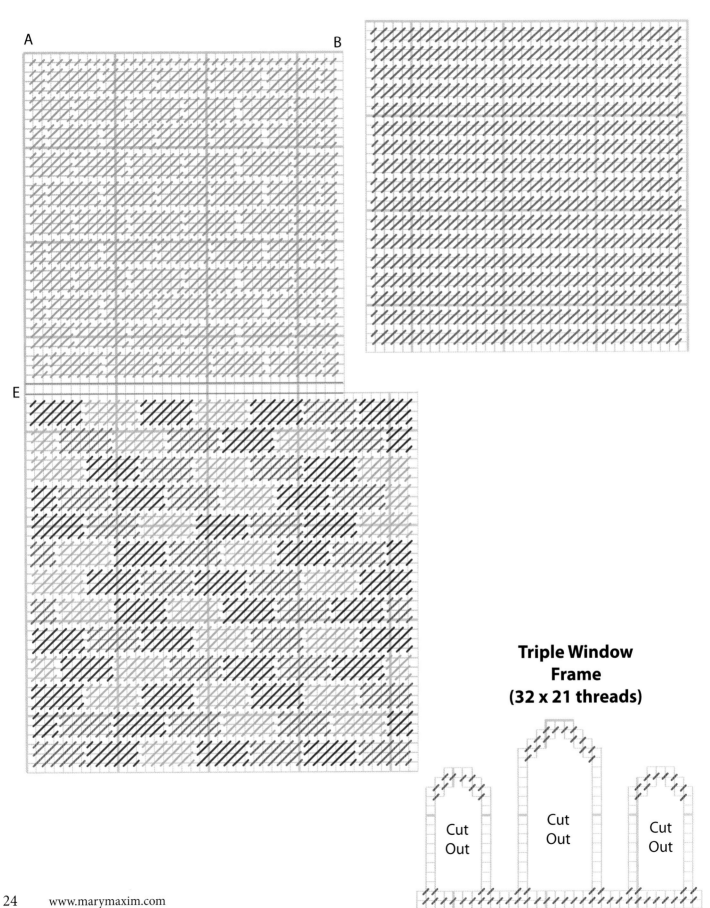

Cut Out

Cut Out

Cut Out

Interior Right Center Wall
(44 x 77 threads)

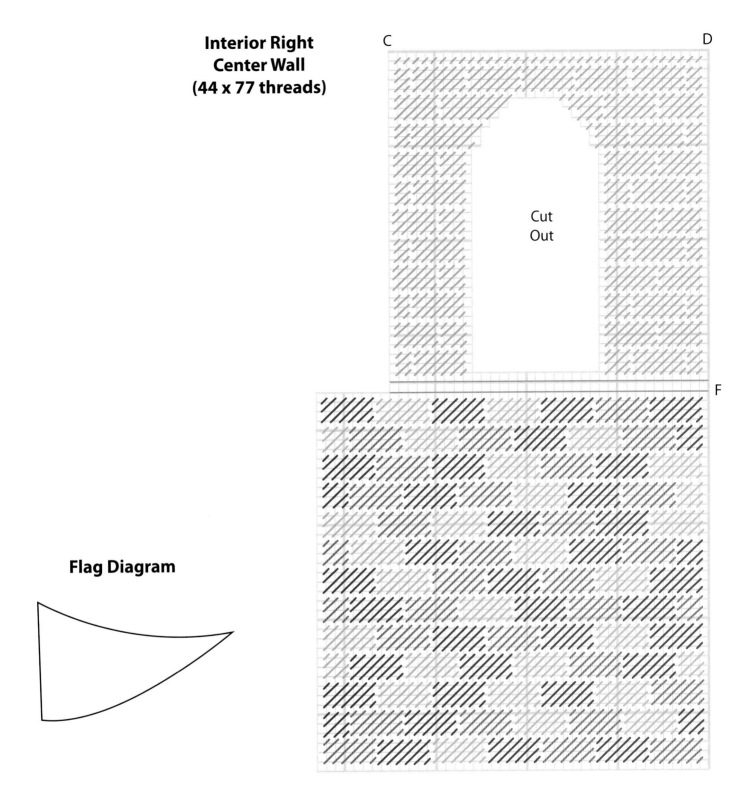

Flag Diagram

Crown Diagram

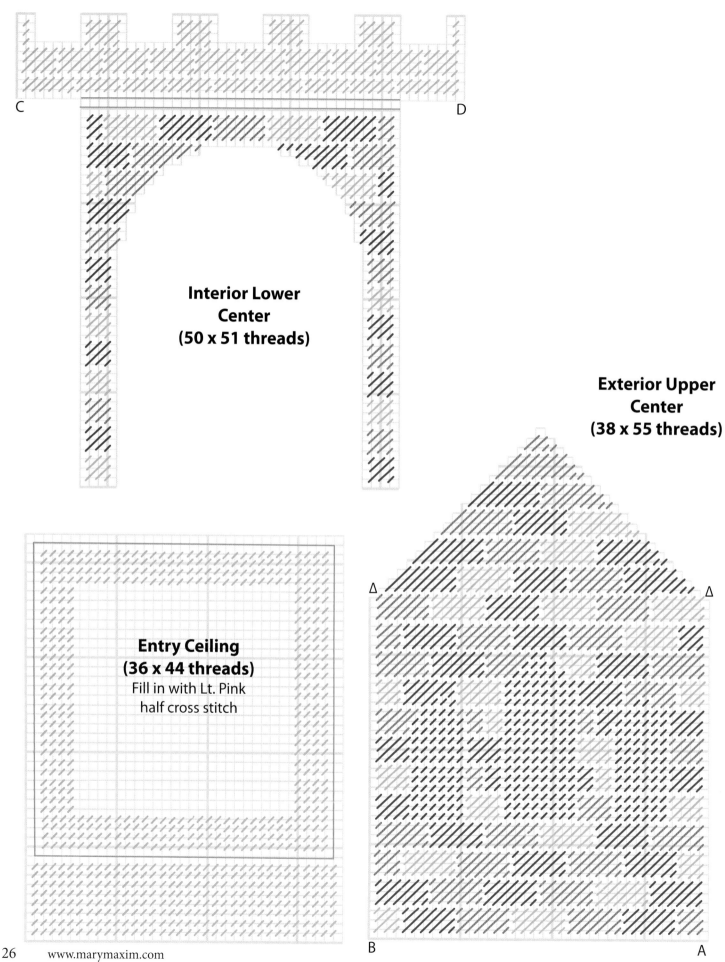

Interior Lower Center
(50 x 51 threads)

Exterior Upper Center
(38 x 55 threads)

Entry Ceiling
(36 x 44 threads)
Fill in with Lt. Pink
half cross stitch

C

D

B

A

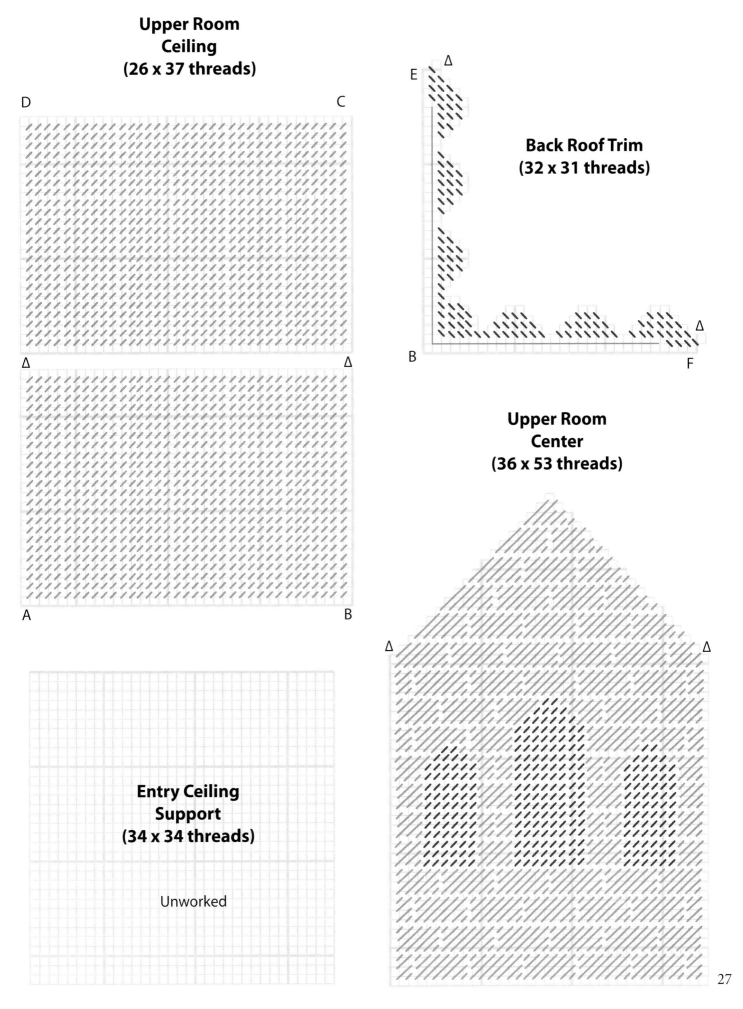

Upper Room Ceiling
(26 x 37 threads)

D

C

Δ

Δ

A

B

Back Roof Trim
(32 x 31 threads)

E

Δ

B

F

Δ

Upper Room Center
(36 x 53 threads)

Δ

Δ

Entry Ceiling Support
(34 x 34 threads)

Unworked

27

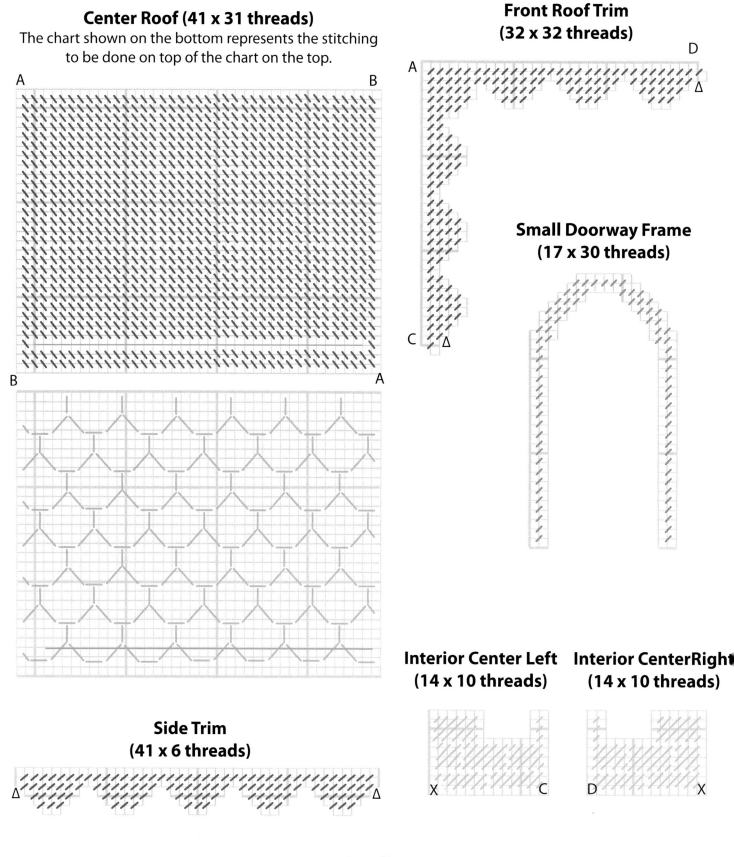

Center Roof (41 x 31 threads)
The chart shown on the bottom represents the stitching to be done on top of the chart on the top.

A   B

B   A

Front Roof Trim
(32 x 32 threads)
A   D

C

Small Doorway Frame
(17 x 30 threads)

Side Trim
(41 x 6 threads)

Interior Center Left
(14 x 10 threads)

X   C

Interior CenterRight
(14 x 10 threads)

D   X

Small Doorway Frame Edge
(60 x 3 threads)

Deck Trim Pieces (13 pieces total)

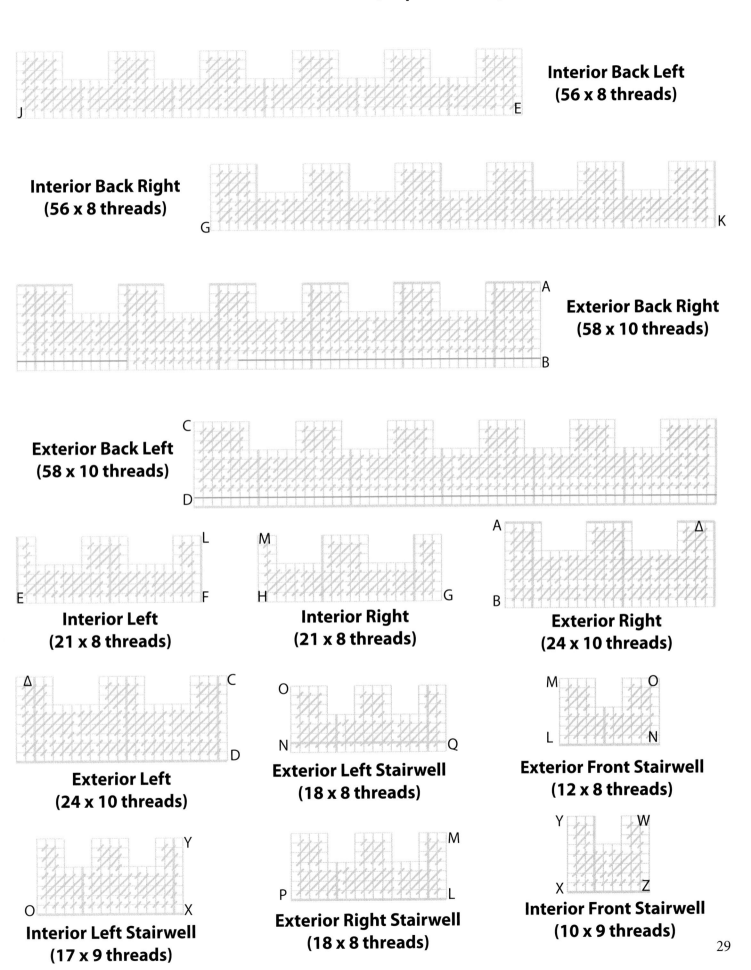

Interior Back Left
(56 x 8 threads)

Interior Back Right
(56 x 8 threads)

Exterior Back Right
(58 x 10 threads)

Exterior Back Left
(58 x 10 threads)

Interior Left
(21 x 8 threads)

Interior Right
(21 x 8 threads)

Exterior Right
(24 x 10 threads)

Exterior Left
(24 x 10 threads)

Exterior Left Stairwell
(18 x 8 threads)

Exterior Front Stairwell
(12 x 8 threads)

Interior Left Stairwell
(17 x 9 threads)

Exterior Right Stairwell
(18 x 8 threads)

Interior Front Stairwell
(10 x 9 threads)

Base Support (146 x 43 threads)

This Base Support chart represents one 146 x 46 thread canvas piece.
It is divided into two sections to make it large enough to be followed easily.

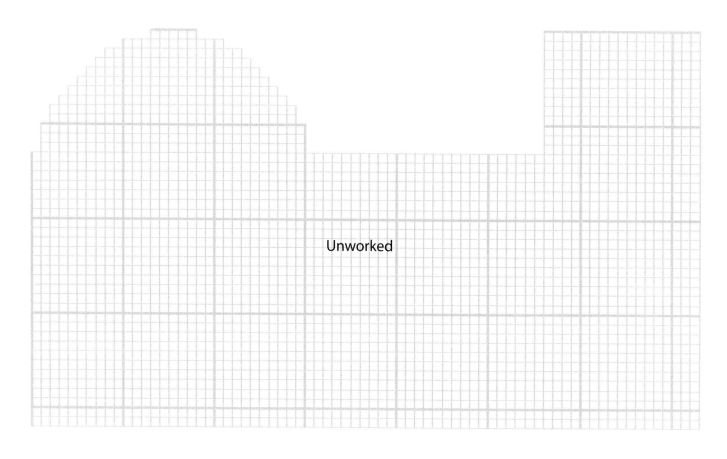

Unworked

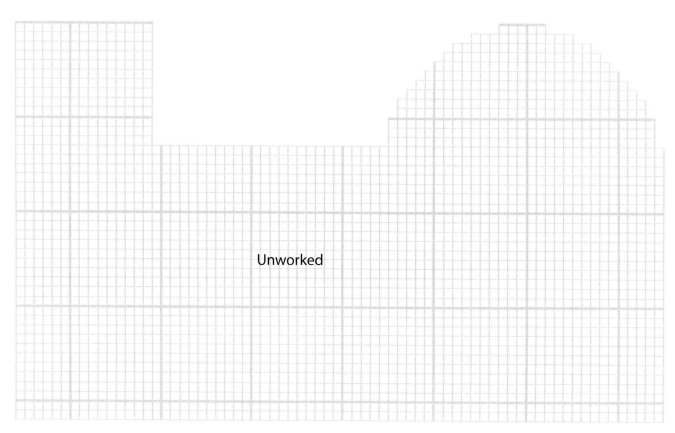

Unworked

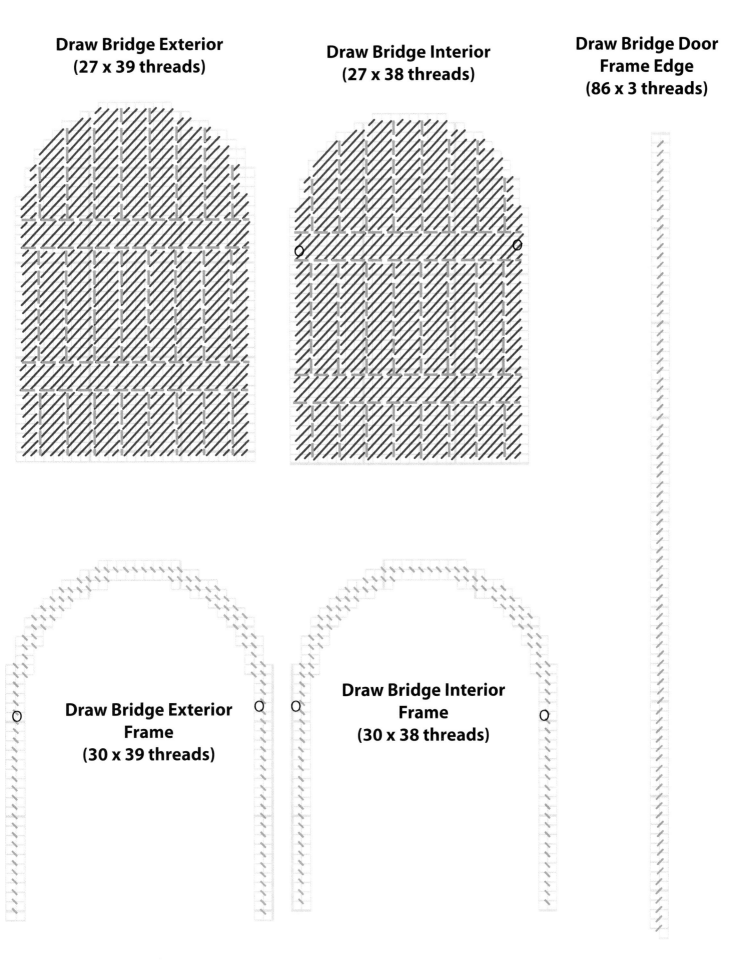

Draw Bridge Exterior
(27 x 39 threads)

Draw Bridge Interior
(27 x 38 threads)

Draw Bridge Door
Frame Edge
(86 x 3 threads)

Draw Bridge Exterior
Frame
(30 x 39 threads)

Draw Bridge Interior
Frame
(30 x 38 threads)

Left Center Support Wall
(34 x 75 threads)

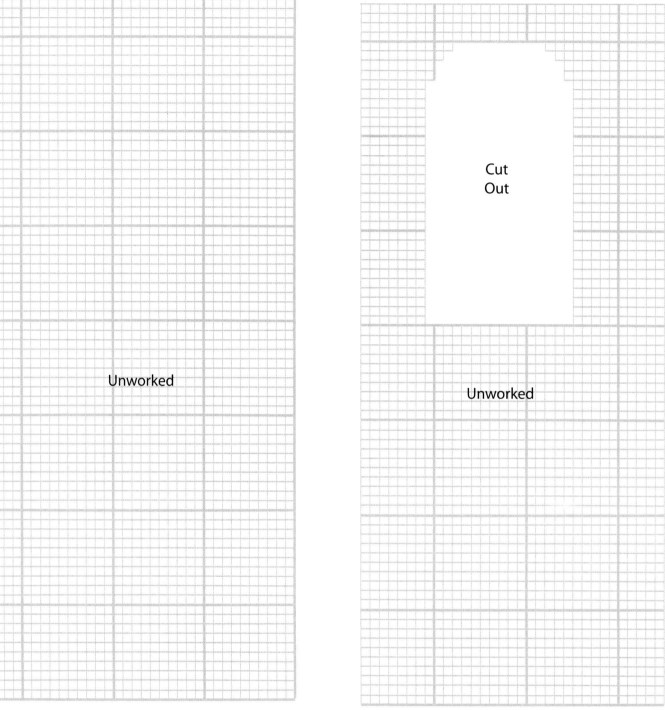

Unworked

Right Center Support Wall
(34 x 75 threads)

Cut
Out

Unworked

Chair Back Legs
(8 x 16 threads)

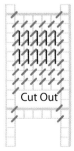

Cut Out

Chair Front Legs
(8 x 8 threads)

Cut Out

Chair Seat
(8 x 6 threads)

Chair Seat Back
(8 x 9 threads)

Chair Side Legs
(7 x 8 threads)

Cut
Out

Small Shrub
(23 x 12 threads)

Large Shrub
(17 x 19 threads)

Table Base
(9 x 9 threads)

Unworked

Table Edge
(63 x 3 threads)

Unworked

Table Top
(3" Circle)

Table Legs
(9 x 12 threads)

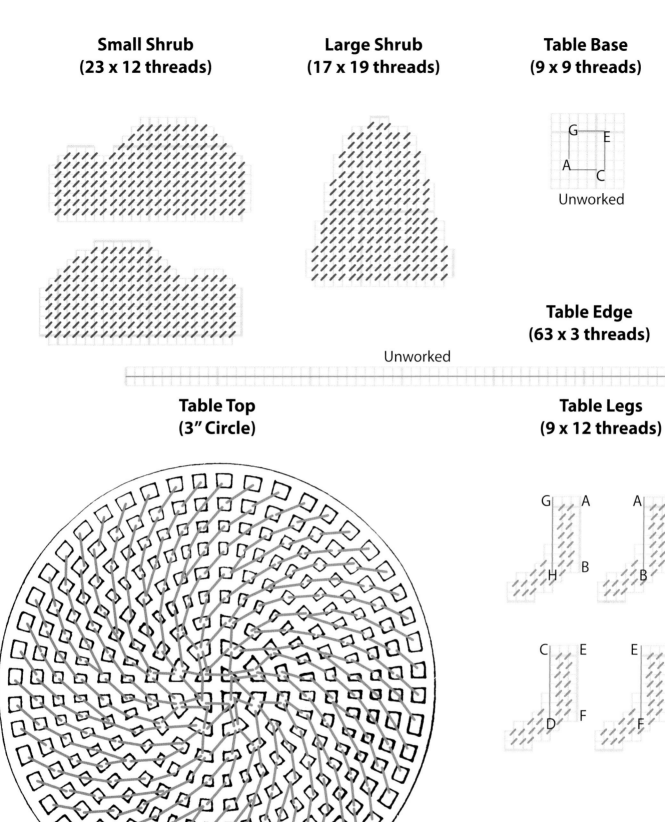

Throne Seat
(7 x 10 threads)

Throne Arm Top
(7 x 2 threads)

Throne Arm
(4 x 7 threads)

Unworked

33

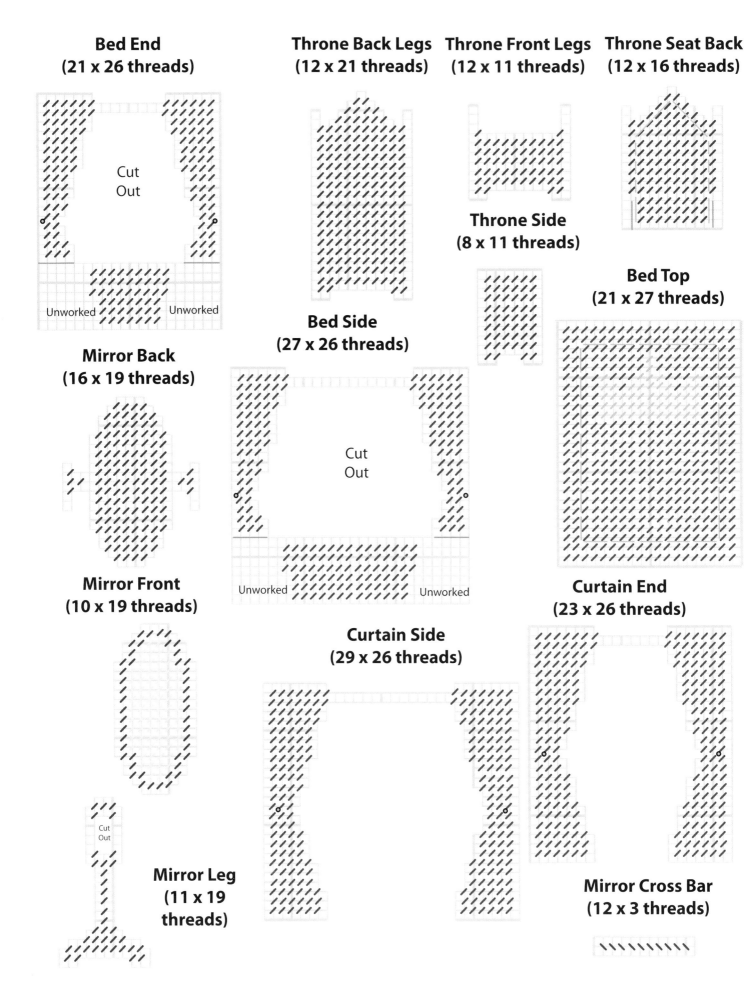

Bed End
(21 x 26 threads)

Cut Out

Unworked   Unworked

Throne Back Legs
(12 x 21 threads)

Throne Front Legs
(12 x 11 threads)

Throne Seat Back
(12 x 16 threads)

Throne Side
(8 x 11 threads)

Bed Top
(21 x 27 threads)

Bed Side
(27 x 26 threads)

Cut Out

Unworked   Unworked

Mirror Back
(16 x 19 threads)

Mirror Front
(10 x 19 threads)

Curtain End
(23 x 26 threads)

Curtain Side
(29 x 26 threads)

Mirror Leg
(11 x 19 threads)

Cut Out

Mirror Cross Bar
(12 x 3 threads)

Fairy Tale Carriage

SIZE:

8.5" x 5" x 8" [21.5 x 12.5 x 20.5 cm]

Please read all instructions included on page 48 before beginning.

INSTRUCTIONS:

This project has a lot of pieces and several are very similar. You may want to cut out just the pieces you'll be working according to the instructions.

Refer to layout diagrams to fit pieces as needed on plastic canvas sheets.

SEATS:

Cut out and work all the seat pieces (pg. 37).

Join a seat top piece to a seat back piece from A to B. Join a seat piece to this seat back piece from C to D. Join a seat front piece to this seat piece from E to F. Divide a length of purple into its individual plies and use 2 plies to work the back stitches and long stitches as shown.

Join a seat side piece to the seat assembly from H to F and from F to D. Overcast the edges from L to D and from D to K. Repeat to join

a seat side to the other end of this seat assembly from G to E and E to C. Overcast the edges from M to C and C to J.

Repeat to create a second seat.

Cut out the floor and floor support pieces. Work the stitches as shown on the floor piece (pg. 43). Using white, join the 4 edges of the unworked support piece to the wrong side of the floor along the joining rows.

Using lavender and working through floor and support, join a seat to each joining row from G to H.

Using white, overcast both sides of the floor between G and H. Using lavender, join the seat side pieces to the floor.

INTERIOR BODY:

Cut out and work the interior body (pg. 38) and the interior top (pg. 37) as shown. Using white, join the ends of the floor piece to the 2 joining rows on the interior piece from L to M.

Using lavender, join the seat tops to the interior body along the joining rows from J to K. Overlap the interior top and the interior body at one end, by one row of holes (matching the X's and O's). Using light pink, work the two rows in half cross stitch to join the pieces together. Repeat to join the other two ends forming a circle.

INTERIOR SIDES:

Cut one outer row and the centers from 2 large circles as shown to make the interior side pieces (pg. 39). Use scraps of yarn to mark the center top and bottom bars. Using

light pink, work the circles in half cross stitch and a few long stitches as needed.

Join the outer edge of each interior side to the interior body (matching top and bottom center bars) with right side of the circles towards the seats.

WHEELS (pg. 40):

Work the 8 small circles for wheels.

Using dark pink and lining up spokes, hold two wheel pieces back to back and overcast their edges, joining to form one wheel. Repeat to make 3 more wheels.

EXTERIOR BODY:

Work the half cross stitches on the exterior body (pg. 41) and exterior top (pg. 39). Using 2 ply of white, work the stars on these two pieces except for the stitches that extend across the unworked rows. Using colors to match stitching, work half cross stitches to join the exterior body and exterior top pieces from A to B and C to D. Finish working the stars.

EXTERIOR SIDES:
Cut out the centers of two large circles as shown for the exterior side pieces (pg. 42). Cut the crown base from one center. Use scraps of yarn to mark top and bottom center bars. Work both pieces as shown. Using dark pink and matching top and bottom center bars, join one exterior side to the exterior body. The second exterior side will be attached later.

Using dark pink, tack 2 wheels to the attached exterior side, see graph for placement. Two rows of medium pink stitching should be visible between wheel edge and center opening in exterior side.

STEPS:
Using purple, work a step and the step ends (pg. 37). Join the ends matching up the triangles. Overcast all edges of this step assembly and tack it to the exterior side where indicated. Repeat to make and attach a step to the other exterior side. Using dark pink, tack the two remaining wheels to this exterior side.

CROWN:
Cut out the crown side piece (pg. 42). Using gold, work the crown side and base pieces. Join the short edges of the crown side piece from Y to Z. Join the edge of the crown base to the unworked row on the crown side piece. Overcast all edges and tack to the top center of the exterior body. Have seam of crown toward front or back of carriage.

DOORS:
Carefully cut the four medium circles as shown for the door pieces (pg. 40). Work each piece in dark pink as shown. Using 2 ply of white, work the stars as shown on two door pieces. These will be exterior door pieces. The two pieces without stars are in the interior door pieces.

Cut out and work two hearts (pg. 42). Using white, overcast all edges of the hearts and tack one on each exterior door between the stars.

Cut out and work two door latch pieces (pg. 43). Overcast all of the edges of both latches. Using dark pink, tack a latch to the right side of one interior door piece and one to left of the other interior door (see black dots on graph for placement). The untacked edge of the latch should extend slightly past the edge of the door piece.

Hold an exterior and an interior door piece back to back. Line up and overcast all edges to join, using dark pink.

CURTAINS:
Use sewing needle and thread while making and attaching the ribbon for curtains on each door. Cut the ribbon in half and use 1 piece for each curtain. Wrap thread around each end of one piece of ribbon to gather tightly. Wrap thread around the center point of the ribbon and then attach to the center top of the opening. Tack the gathered ends to the bottom of the opening at each side, folding under the cut ends. Repeat to make second curtain.

Center a door on the attached exterior side. Using dark pink, join the door to the exterior side at the hinge area, opposite side from the latch. Work the stitches over the outer edge of the door and keep them just loose enough to work as a hinge. Attach the second door to the other exterior side piece. Latch and hinge placement should be reversed so that both doors will open towards the same end of the carriage when finished.

Secure two full lengths of dark pink near the bottom center bar of the exterior piece. Secure a full length of medium pink to each interior side piece, near the center opening. Remove the yarn scraps from one interior side piece. Slide the interior pieces into the exterior pieces lining up center bars. Remove the yarn scraps marking the center bars. Join the edges of the center openings of the interior and exterior side pieces. Place remaining exterior side on the carriage, line up top and bottom center bars and remove yarn scraps. Join the exterior body and side pieces together. Join the edges of the center openings of the interior and exterior side pieces.

Layout Diagrams

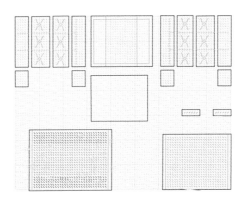
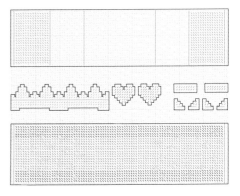

Seat Top
(6 x 21 threads)

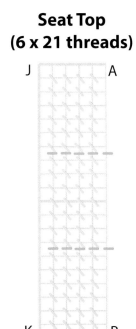

Seat Back
(8 x 21 threads)

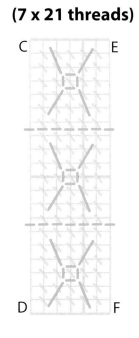

Seat
(7 x 21 threads)

Seat Front
(6 x 21 threads)

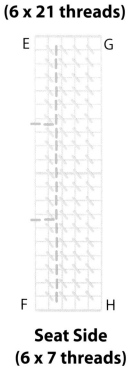

Seat Side
(6 x 7 threads)

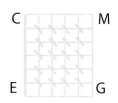

Seat Side
(6 x 7 threads)

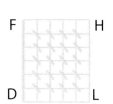

Interior Top
(29 x 23 threads)

Center

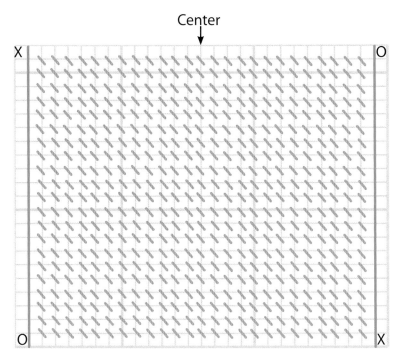

Step
(10 x 4 threads)

Step Ends
(5 x 5 threads)

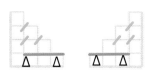

37

Interior Body (91 x 23 threads)

This Interior Body chart represents one 91 x 23 thread canvas piece.
It is divided into two sections to make it large enough to be followed easily.

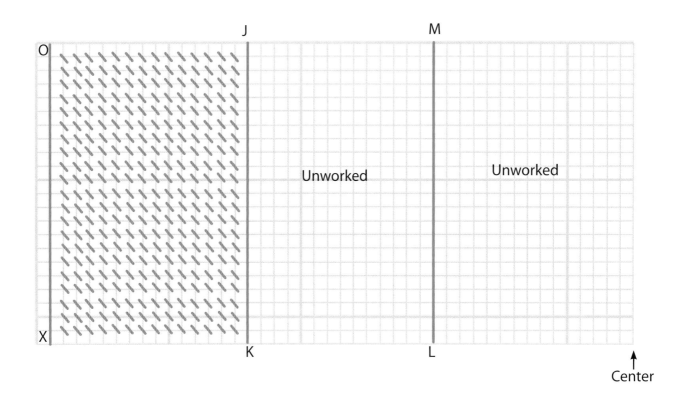

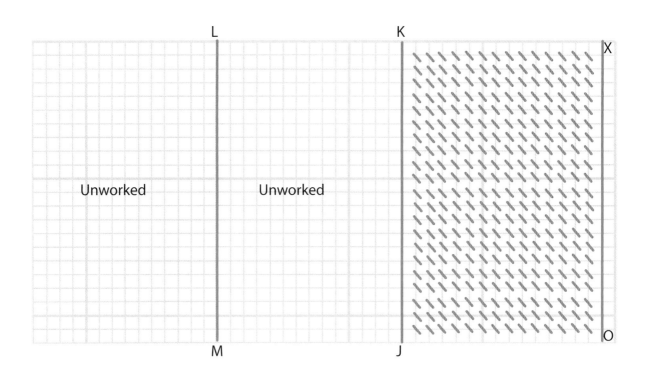

**Interior Side
(Large Circles)**

Center

CUT
OUT

Center

**Exterior Top
(35 x 25 threads)**

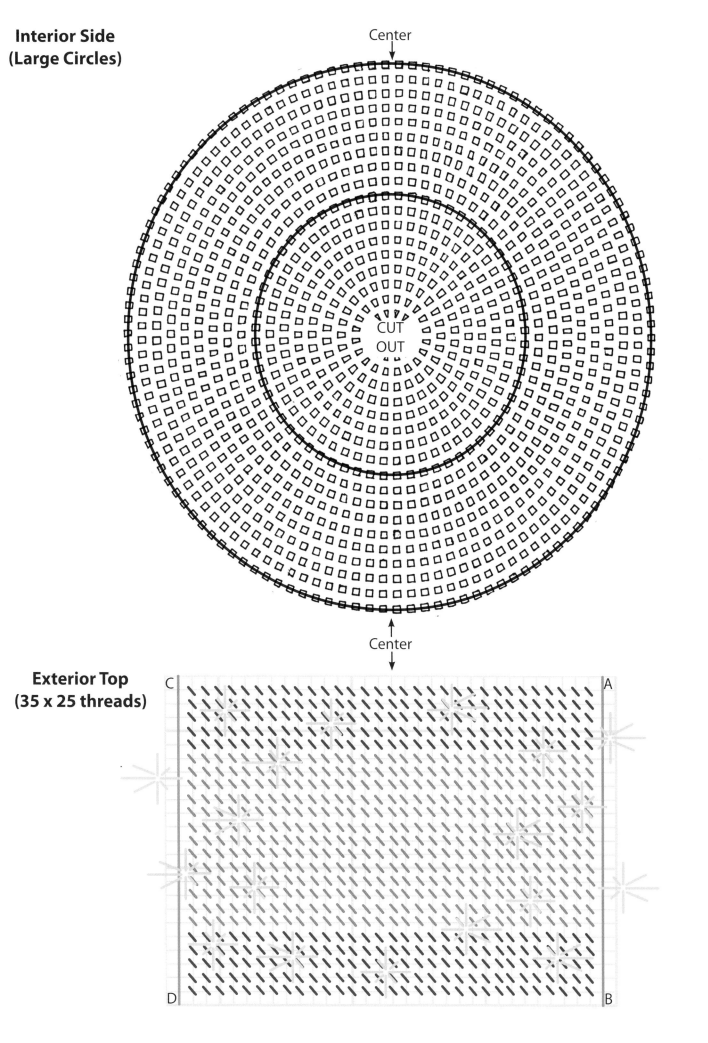

C

A

D

B

39

**Wheels
(Small Circles)**

**Doors
(Medium Circles)**

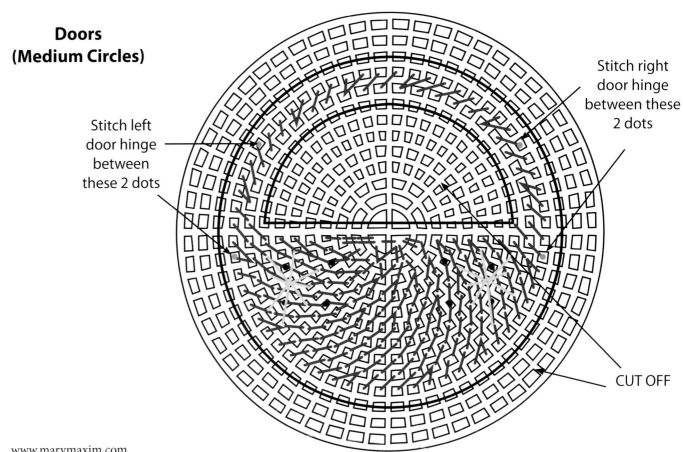

Stitch left
door hinge
between
these 2 dots

Stitch right
door hinge
between these
2 dots

CUT OFF

Exterior Body (91 x 25 threads)

This Exterior Body chart represents one 91 x 25 thread canvas piece. It is divided into two sections to make it large enough to be followed easily. No threads or stitches are repeated from one piece to the next.

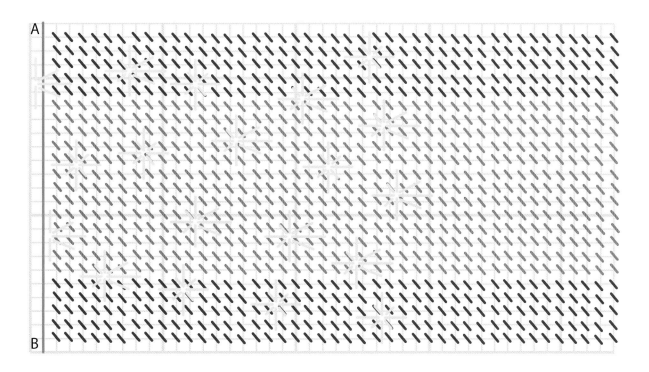

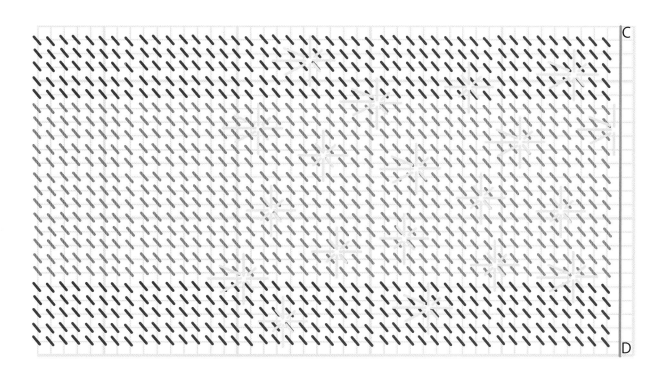

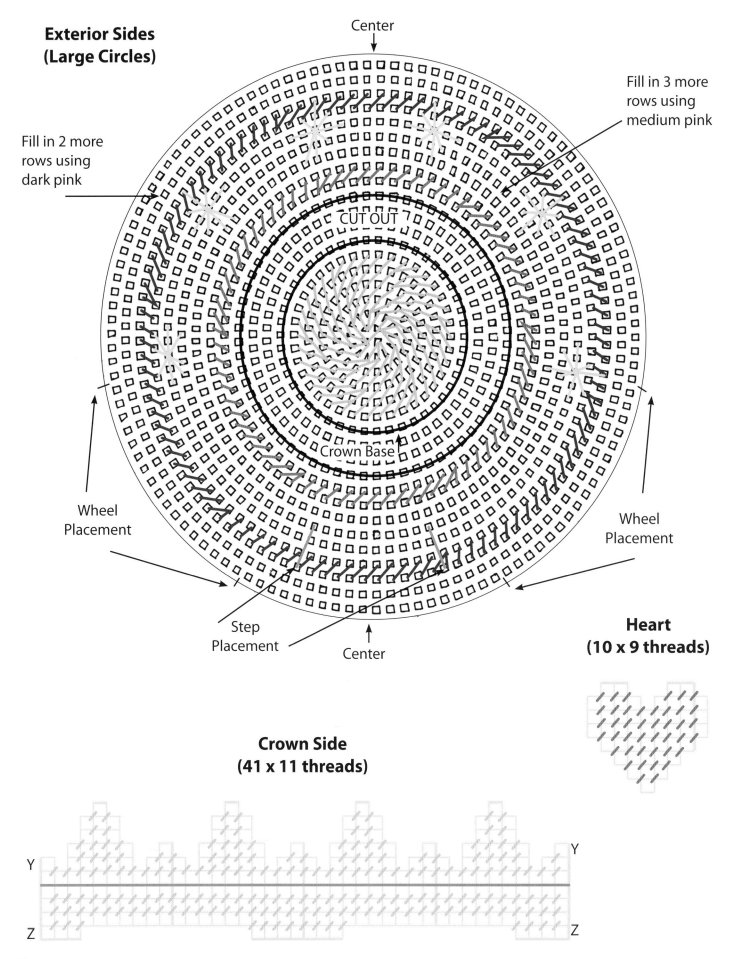

Exterior Sides
(Large Circles)

Center

Fill in 3 more
rows using
medium pink

Fill in 2 more
rows using
dark pink

CUT OUT

Crown Base

Wheel
Placement

Wheel
Placement

Step
Placement

Center

Heart
(10 x 9 threads)

Crown Side
(41 x 11 threads)

Y

Y

Z

Z

Floor
(26 x 21 threads)

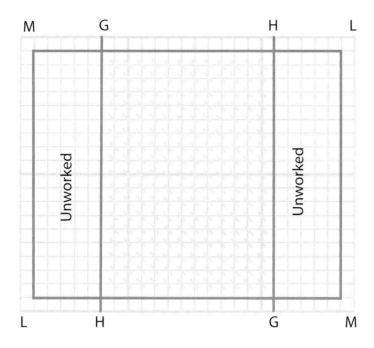

Floor Support
(24 x 19 threads)

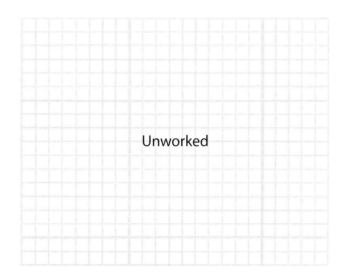

Door Latch
(8 x 3 threads)

Fairy Tale Crown and Wand

SHOPPING LIST

- ☐ Worsted weight yarn (refer to master key below)
- ☐ Tapestry Needle #18
- ☐ 1- Pink 7 Mesh Plastic Canvas 11" x 14"
- ☐ 5/8" Lavender Ribbon 2 yds
- ☐ 1/8" Pink Ribbon 1/2 yd
- ☐ 1/8" Purple Ribbon 1/2 yd
- ☐ 1/4" Dowel 12" long
- ☐ 17-Pink 10mm Round Rhinestones
- ☐ 18-Dk. Amethyst 7mm Rhinestones
- ☐ 1- 25 x 18mm True Amethyst Rhinestone

SIZE:

Crown:
13.5" x 4" [34.5 x 10 cm]
Wand:
13" [33 cm] long

Please read all instructions included on page 48 before beginning.
Hot glue or jewelry glue will work well for the rhinestones. You may wish to leave the large rhinestone off the crown for a child under 3 years of age.

INSTRUCTIONS:

Refer to layout diagram (pg. 47) to fit pieces as needed on plastic canvas sheet.

CROWN:

Cut out the front and back pieces (pgs. 45 & 46). Cut out the narrow slits and holes as indicated on the front. Cut out the holes on the back piece. Work the half cross stitches as shown on the crown front. (The background of the front and the entire back are unworked.)

Cut a 42" [106.5 cm] length of lavender (wide) ribbon. Thread the ribbon across the bottom of the crown front piece as follows:
Starting at one end, thread the ribbon through the first slit from front to back.
Bring the ribbon to the front though the next slit, over the single bar marked X and return to the back.
Repeat at the following 3 X's.
Bring the ribbon back to the front through the slit at the end. Center the ribbon so equal lengths are on each side. Trim ends on an angle.

Place the crown back behind the crown front.
Using light pink, work overcast stitches to join the 2 pieces together along the bottom, the top edges and around the 4 upper cut out holes.

Glue the rhinestones to the crown as shown on the graph.

Tie ribbon ends of the crown to fit your princess.

WAND:

Cut out 2 stars (pg. 47). Work the heart on both stars, one in medium pink and one in purple. Fill in the background of each star with half cross stitches in the opposite color.
Glue rhinestones on each star as shown.

Using medium pink, overcast the small section of each star from A to B.

Place the stars together back to back and work an overcast stitch around all unworked edges using medium pink.

Thread the purple narrow ribbon through one star at the X. Center the ribbon and tie to hold. Repeat with the pink ribbon on the other star.

Glue one end of the remaining lavender ribbon to the top end of the dowel at an angle.
Wrap the ribbon around the dowel spiraling downward and overlapping slightly to cover the dowel completely.

Glue in a few places as you work. Glue securely at the bottom.

Leave the ribbon tail at a desired length at bottom and trim end on an angle.

Push top of dowel up into the opening at the center bottom of the star.

Master Key

╱	Med. Pink - 16 yds
╱	Dk. Pink - 4 yds
╱	Purple - 4 yds

Rhinestones

⬤	Purple Oval
◯	Pink
●	Small Purple

Crown Back (91 x 31 threads)

This Crown Back chart represents one 91 x 31 thread canvas piece.
It is divided into two sections to make it large enough to be followed easily.
No threads are repeated from one piece to the next.

Unworked

Unworked

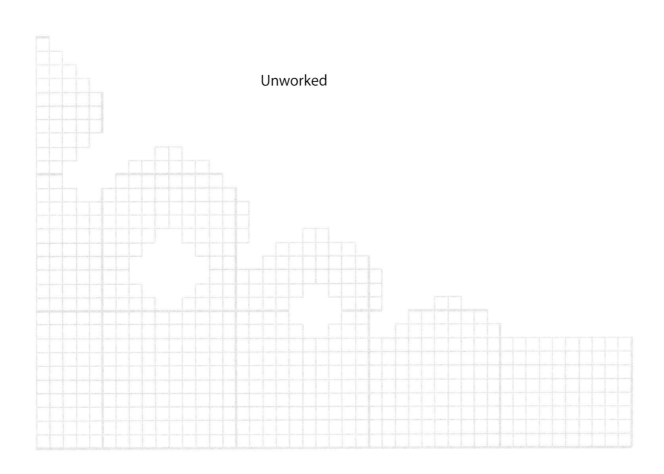

Crown Front (91 x 31 threads)

This Crown Front chart represents one 91 x 31 thread canvas piece.
It is divided into two sections to make it large enough to be followed easily.
No threads or stitches are repeated from one piece to the next.

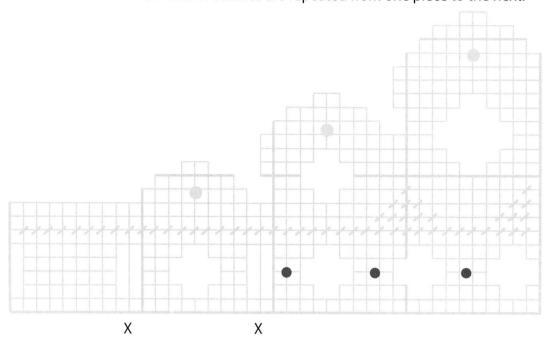

X   X

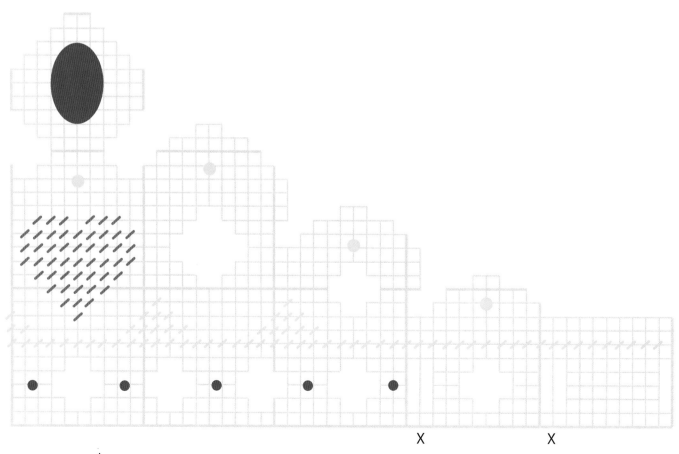

X   X

Star
(34 x 33 threads)

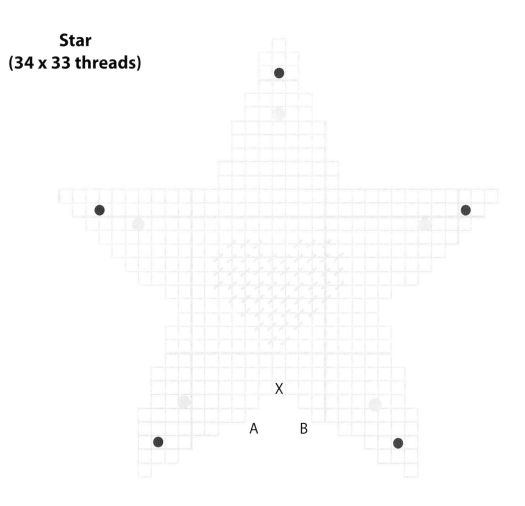

X

A   B

Layout Diagram

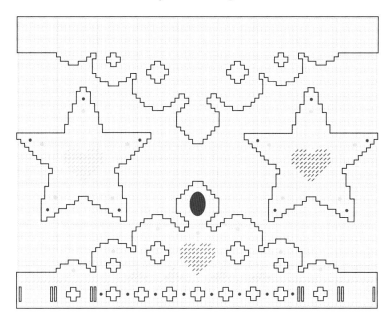

General Instructions

NOTE:

Please read all of the instructions before beginning. When joining pieces, refer to photos and notice whether right side of stitching should face in or out. You may need to use a few common household items to complete your project.

GENERAL INSTRUCTIONS:

Cutting the canvas must be done very carefully. If you miscut, the piece is ruined and you'll have to cut another piece. Our graphs show the shape of the pieces when they are cut out, making it easier for you to follow the cutting line. To cut, count bars, not holes. On each graph we show the total maximum number of bars required for each piece. (If you find it necessary to mark on canvas, use a pencil, but use it cautiously as the yarn will pick up the marks.) Plastic canvas is hand washable but do not put it in the dryer and do not dry clean. Cut in the space between the bars (as shown on the graph) rather than on a bar. After cutting, you will need to trim off all plastic nubs that remain to give your work a more finished look.

STITCHING INSTRUCTIONS:

Using 1 yard pieces of yarn, keep an even tension, making sure canvas is completely covered. However, too tight a tension will cause the canvas to curl. Work row across, first from left to right, then returning from right to left. To begin strand, draw needle though canvas until about 1/2" [1 cm] remains at back. Hold this end close to canvas and catch it in stitches on reverse side of work. To end each strand, put needle through to back and draw under a few stitches to secure. Trim yarn close to work. All joining rows and indicated areas are unworked.

Stitches

Half Cross Stitch

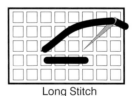

Long Stitch

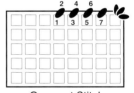

Overcast Stitch

Backstitch

French Knot

Lazy Daisy

EVERY EFFORT HAS BEEN MADE TO HAVE THE DIRECTIONS CONTAINED IN THESE PATTERNS ACCURATE AND COMPLETE; HOWEVER, WE CANNOT BE RESPONSIBLE FOR MISINTERPRETATION, VARIANCE OR ERRORS IN WORKMANSHIP OF THE INDIVIDUAL.